Garibaldi's Legs
poems
Fiona Ritchie Walker

First published 2005 by IRON Press
5 Marden Tce, Cullercoats, North Shields, Northumberland
England, NE30 4PD
Tel/Fax: +44 (0) 191 253 1901
Email: seaboy@freenetname.co.uk
website: www.ironpress.co.uk
ISBN 0 906228 96 4

© Fiona Ritchie Walker 2005

Typeset in Times New Roman
Pagesetting, layout and cover design by Kate Jones

Printed by Tyneside Free Press,
Charlotte Square, Newcastle upon Tyne

IRON Press is a member of Independent Northern Publishers

IRON Press books are distributed by Central Books
and represented by
Inpress Ltd, Northumberland House,
11 The Pavement, Popes Lane, Ealing,
London W5 4NG
Tel: +44 (0)20 8832 7464
Fax: +44 (0)20 8832 7465
Email: stephanie@inpressbooks.co.uk
Web: www.inpressbooks.co.uk

Fiona Ritchie Walker

Fiona Ritchie Walker is originally from Montrose, Angus, but has lived in North East England since the early 1990s. Her first collection *Lip Reading* was published by Diamond Twig and her poetry and short stories have been published in many magazines and anthologies, including *New Writing 11* (British Council/Picador), *Bracket* (Comma Press) and *New Writing Scotland*.

Acknowledgements

Some of these poems have appeared in *First Eleven, Mslexia, Other Poetry, Rain Dog, Riverrun, Sand, Second Light, Smiths Knoll, Under Your Skin, Wild Cards,* on the *Franks Casket* and *Diamond Twig* websites, and in the Barnet Open Poetry and Lancaster Litfest competition anthologies.

'Small Things I Have Slept With' was commissioned by New Writing North as part of Magnetic North.

Thanks to Dr Robert Dunn for insight into the lives of dust mites and to New Writing North for a Northern Promise Award in 2004. To Jeanne Macdonald and Heather Young, love and special thanks.

For David

Contents

9	2am
10	Typecast
11	Sasine
12	The Main Course
13	Pomegranate
14	Meeting the Congregation
16	Confession
17	Practising for the Dance
19	Sleep Over
20	One in Four
22	Filling the Kettle
23	Stranger Still
31	Continents
32	Word-hoard
33	Anna C
34	A Scot Moves South
35	Coda
37	Adorned
38	After Life

40	Jericho
41	Garibaldi's Legs
42	19:28 to Newcastle
44	Sleeping With My Lover
45	Beyond Durban
47	Wrong Timing
49	On the Factory Floor
50	Small Things I Have Slept With
52	Tie-dyed T-shirt
54	Estuary Island
55	Girls I Like
57	Strip
58	The Language of Birds
59	Night-time Breathing
60	45 Not Out
61	Last Request

2am

This should still be party hour,
her skipping home, carrying her shoes,
giggles rising to tickle the stars.
She should be wiping away mascara
not dabbing leaking nipples.

Sleep is a taut key.
She's fully wound and waiting
for that thin wail that triggers milk,
sets clockwork legs in motion,
turning stitches to splinters.

Her heart pounds until he latches on,
gulps himself into silence.
The girl with the tired eyes stares from the mirror.
She wonders who she is,
why she is smiling.

Typecast

      you can use your own keys
open unknown doors   close them

turn white to black   strike
    something new

      you can create worlds
                destroy them

you   can be unfaithful   foreign
      you can be the opposite sex

      you can make the past
another planet

the future   present tense

      in your parallel universe
there can be
    can be a happy ending

      what you don't want
you kiss to death with crosses   backspace

Fiona Ritchie Walker

Sasine

I cut my hand and out comes the River Esk
turned red by the sun setting over the glen of a knuckle,
my river pooling into Celurca's sea loch
and if I had a stone I'd be skimming it.

I look for the source, follow with my finger
the strange hummocking of vein under skin,
my own brown and white Caterthuns,
the Pictish landmarks of raised moles
mapping cup and ring.

Here is my silver scar
memorial to ancient battlefields.

Over the brae of a bare shoulder lies my sandstone jawbone,
milky Lunan dunes. The path along my Angus coastline
carries a warning of ancient quarrying
for minerals and semi-precious stones,
follows arteries round limbs and drumlin hollows
to reach my volcanic core.
Hidden, dirling, simmering.

sasine – transfer of ancient land rights in Scotland
dirling – quivering, tingling

The Main Course

Today you are Cape Malay,
enticing me with spices,
your rich sauce blending with
the Knysna pot. From your fingers
come fennel, cinnamon and coriander,
an earthy rainbow dipping down
to your dish of burnished gold.

Slowly, throughout the day,
you are simmering for me.

When the sun is pulsing amber
in an evening sky, you will let
this aromatic dew, full of butter-rich
brinjies and capsicums, pour
upon my white rice; it will spread
dark upon my china and seep
into the yeast holes of my torn bread,
your taste lingering on my burning lips
until morning.

Fiona Ritchie Walker

Pomegranate

That night he called her princess.
Next day in the market she bought him
the best from Azerbaijan, found a perfect fruit,
crowned with the prettiest calyx.

Waiting for the train
she gave him her pomegranate,
watched him touch the scarlet blush,
run slim fingers over its body.

Walking home she wills him
to remember Babylon,
those first fruits
found in the hanging garden,
pictures him
breaking open the shining husk,
reaching
that rosy, sweet-seeded centre,
letting
perfumed juices burst between his lips.

In her bedsit
she will count the days
with pomegranate seeds,
watch them dry
in the winter sun,
force herself to taste
the bitter yellow membrane.

Meeting the Congregation

My ability to name body parts
has shocked you. I can see it
in your faces. Being his wife
you want me to unfold
a crisp, linen cloth, place it
over all flesh. But in our house
nothing is ironed.

I know, it's not what you expected.
the hunks of bread, those mugs,
the unmade bed. You wanted something
inkeeping with his collar
and I am too familiar,
hanging scant lace on the line,
relaxed that my children
have seen me naked.

He seems so nice, I know,
and you long for us to be
a matching pair,
me baking scones,
his strong hands to lift the urn

Fiona Ritchie Walker

but he likes the touch of my body
and the smell and taste
of being together,
knowing
that we don't care –
the bedroom, the kitchen,
the blinds not down.
Even with the lights on.

Confession

Sometimes
in the middle of a sermon
I choose a word
redemption sin salvation
any one will do

and each time you say it
I remove
shoe sock shirt
until I see you in the pulpit
wearing a collar
and the ring I slipped on your finger

which is fine
except
when I miss that last *amen*
making you carry your books
and your nakedness
down the central aisle
past all those old ladies.

Fiona Ritchie Walker

Practising for the Dance

We are waltzing St Bernard-style.
Side together, side together, side and lower

sixty four gym shoes scuff across the floor,
scratchy vinyl spins, Mr Burness bellows monotone

and back for two, and in for two,
out for two, turn the lady round once

and one two three, one two three
ready to start again.

Alphabetically paired, Walker and Waller.
My silent scream at the touch of your warts,
your Primary 5 smile. We ease
into each other's rhythm, Gay Gordons
double quick, the class favourite.

No giggling at the back, pairs in a circle please.
We heel-toe our way into a Canadian barn.

Bounce kick, bounce kick
turn the lady round

waltzing one two three, one two three
ready to start again.

Garibaldi's Legs

I grow used to the touch of your arm,
start to hum along close to your ear
until the music stops and we spin separately
through the seasons to Primary 6

waltzing one two three, one two three
ready to start again.

Fiona Ritchie Walker

Sleep Over

They had brought America with them.
Their Hershey bars and root beer,
their own language.

In the American school
at the foot of the Angus glens
they were taught a different history.

The day my parents were guests at the US Navy Ball
I stayed overnight and ate cheese squeezed from a bottle.
I read *The Cat in the Hat* for the very first time.

Charlene suggested ice cream, laughed
when I ran out listening for the chimes of the van
while she opened up the icebox.

One in Four

*(In the early 1970s, it was planned that one in four
teenage schoolgirls in Scotland would attend talks on
how to prepare for a nuclear attack)*

Three still think of boys when they walk home from school tonight,
stopping in Boots to buy shimmering lip gloss,
hoping for a free spray of Aqua Manda.

>One sits cross-legged on the gym floor,
>varnished wood cold against bare legs,
>waits for the woman to speak.

It's Thursday. Top of the Pops.
Linda says T Rex should still be number one.
She wants to marry Marc Bolan.

>*Welcome girls to One in Four,
>a talk to equip the young women of Scotland.
>You are specially chosen to receive this information.*

When Linda waves goodbye to Lorna and Sue,
opens her front door, she never thinks
about which rooms in her house have no outside walls.

>*Preparation now could mean survival in the future.*

At the newsagents, Sue buys this week's Jackie.
She and Lorna pour over Cathy and Clare's problem page,
read remedies for greasy hair and blackheads.

Fiona Ritchie Walker

> *Whitewashed walls will help to repel radiation.*
> *You must build up a stock of tinned food and candles,*
> *keep blankets and buckets at the ready.*

They walk past the new houses
never noticing the sliding glass doors
which will shatter when the blinding light arrives.

> *Make a mental note of where your family should gather.*
> *A cupboard under the stairs may offer best protection.*
> *Buy batteries. The radio will be your lifeline.*

Sue says the girl next door is getting married.
She has seen through cracks in the bedroom curtains,
thinks they may have done 'it'.

> *No-one knows the long-term effects.*
> *Slow death for some,*
> *the unborn may suffer blindness or mutation.*

One in four stops in Boots on the way home,
nicks a pack of three. Knows a lad who'll help her
make the best of four minutes tonight.

Filling the Kettle

You must find a thinning, a darker blue.
Raise the axe high above you.
Pretend the frozen lake is a moose head
or your oldest enemy.

You must pull the icy air sharp into your lungs.
Stretch your arms high.
Feel the cold like a knife, begin to hate
the weight of the metal above you.

Like an eagle weigh up distance.
The secret is confidence,
knowing the blade will land heavy,
will cut, not splinter.

You must build up a rhythm.
Soon you will not feel the bite
of each breath, the pain in your shoulders.
Soon you will see the glint of arctic waters.

Fiona Ritchie Walker

Stranger Still

Hitch

A thrill hits her in the heat of the cab.
Not the sandpaper touch
of the truck driver's hand,

the feeling of being anonymous.
A word springs up in the rhythm
of the ride. Alone.

Sacramento

The dollars in her pocket
are starting to make sense,

the patterned soles of her shoes
are thinning. Every day

she follows the road
to another name. She is lured

by rich vowels, anything
with the letter S.

Garibaldi's Legs

Bruise

Last night she dreamt of the flats,
her father brawling with auld Archie,
milk bottles sprawled along the landing.

She saw herself peering through the banisters,
smelt her mother's closeness, that musty mix:
unwashed underwear, fags and fake Chanel.

She wanted to be somewhere clean.
She thought it would be called America.

Somewhere

There was no blinding flash, no sudden change.
Somewhere along the road it grew into a highway,

the dripping tap turned to faucet,
her poke of chips became a bag of fries.

Her oxters still stink from days of travelling.
She still wakes with a damp Scottish cough.

Somewhere on her journeying
she threw away her name.

Fiona Ritchie Walker

Neon

She is thinking of Las Vegas,
wants to live in a room with
the comforting blink of bright neon.

Hotel, Motel, All-nite Bar –
the words don't matter
but she must have peacock blue

like the eyes of the man beside her.
For him she was Carla.
She will remember him:

the fattest wallet in a week,
ten days' travel, new jeans
and 60 cents change.

Francoise

All along she's said she doesn't do girls.

Six hours of neighbouring thighs
on a sticky bus, eventually
they share smiles.

When the girl speaks
her breath is a vanilla butterfly,
her consonants build to the Eiffel Tower.

Something beautiful to be scaled.

Motel

Clean skin makes them hungry. She feels
the lash of wet hair on her shoulder,
runs fingers through damp hollows. They make
a midnight sandwich, sweetly filled.

Dawn

More than trying on, more
than a laugh, an easy
mistake, picking up
the wrong bra
fresh from the line.

More than the g-string, more
than the way it makes
her back arch up.
More than anything
she wants to be Her.

Fiona Ritchie Walker

Fork

The map they picked from an old man's pocket
lies on the table. She follows Francoise' finger.

"Why change something good?"
It's her own voice yelling.

Her hand spills the coffee,
her whole body shaking,

She wants to keep going,
no fork in the road. No parting.

Negative

Film ribbons from the camera,
exposed and destroyed.
She will still burn it.

Eyelids like shutters, she tries to sleep.
She remembers the climb
but nothing of the view.

She remembers posing for pictures,
the words, the tears,
their disagreement.

She remembers her hands,
the ravine, the push.
The silence.

Merge

She makes her selection.
Jeans, lipstick, perfume,
passport and signature.
Broken English.

Sam

She is alone and heading for the bus.
She doesn't feel the fingers
unzip her bag, doesn't see
the boy slope off down the alley,
the man who follows.

She only hears the shouting,
turns to receive
the recovered passport.
It feels electric when he
touches her hand.

"Qui, monsieur. Je m'appelle
Francoise. Merci."

Fiona Ritchie Walker

Moving In

She tells herself she stays
because of the sunrise,
the view from Sam's studio window,
the coffee he makes which tastes so good.

Later there will be time for travelling.

He tells her she is beautiful.
He is teaching her English between
long, deep kisses and nights
of drinking and eating each other.

Later she'll find the right time to tell him.

She watches him with the brush.
The way he moves his hand, pressing
pigment on paper sends ripples
deep inside her. He keeps asking
her to pose, but each time
she undresses, the brush
falls from his fingers,
the light changes.

Remembering 2C

Miss McDonald's bluebottle voice flew around the room,
bounced off the Alps and Mont St Michel,
hit the blackboard with its feminine endings,

rested on her shoulders, turned into a request
for translation. She read easily. Miss McDonald smiled.
"You're a natural, so you are."

Recipe

'France and its People.'
'A Guide to Pregnancy.'
'Cordon Bleu Made Easy.'

The library aisles
hold all that she needs
to make things work.

Fiona Ritchie Walker

Continents

He dreamt of Craster kippers and all things Northumbrian.
Once he saw Lindisfarne in clouds above the Golden Gate.
He searched San Francisco for Newcastle Brown
              though it never touched his lips at home.

I sent Kathryn Tickell in a padded bag, the Angel of the North
went airmail, with recipes for stottie and singin' hinnie.
I declared two bags of black bullets.

When he returned, he asked for bourbon. At midnight,
in candlelight, I lay on smooth linen, hair harvest gold,
eyes the colour of Keilder. He moaned about the cold,

spoke of cities never sleeping, nights on fire. The taste
of another continent kissed my lips as rhythmic bodies
recreated the San Andreas Fault, prayed for an earthquake.

Word-hoard

When they broke down our door
they found her trying to eat the evidence,
adjectives slipping down her chin,
some with capitals had caught in her cleavage.

All her pockets were slippy with vowels. Later
there would be rumours she'd been breeding them.
The sergeant wanted to charge her with onomatopoeia,
opted instead for lewd and libidinous language.

When they strip-searched her, a whole bucket
of pronouns was taken away as evidence.
Her trial was in camera, not one syllable escaped.
Waiting for the verdict, I felt apostrophied.

She's doing six months in solitary, cell sluiced out daily:
too many verbs mushrooming. I long for her release.
The proper nouns have taken over the kitchen
and sharing a home with so many italics leaves me hyphenated.

Anna C

Too much to drink, too tired to undress
I lie with my belt buckled, dreaming
of emerald eyes, sleek muscles in a waterfall;
wake with Yanos on my lips.

Trevor says my tongue's like fire
darting round his teeth. He bought me
the shoes, yellow and brown. They fit
like a second skin; I glide through puddles.

I like the matching bag, stroke its scales
on the bus and think of palm swamps.
Now I've stopped eating, I pull the belt tighter.
It patterns my skin, mottling nicely now.

In this rain I long for Amazon shores.
Thinking like this makes me hungry. I sidle
up to Trev, give him such a hug he yells.
I can hear my stomach gurgling.

A Scot Moves South

Sometimes an *och* sneaks south of the border,
it hitches a ride on a telephone line. Brings with it
a blether wearing a simmet, scratching an itchy oxter.
In its bag a sair heedie, horniegoloch and a bridie.
But it can't go swimming. No dookers.

I'll swap you a sea fret and a bag of ket for a haar
and some grannie sookers. But I'll keep plodging,
nithering and bottoming, starting my sentences
with *ee* to show there's no animosity
between us border traders.

Fiona Ritchie Walker

Coda

I played this first for Rudolph Valentino,
a far cry from accompanying Mr Dodd,
shuffling round, grabbing breasts and bottoms as he passes.
I'm safe on the piano stool, he forgets I'm here
though I anticipate his every movement,
slow down the notes when he lowers himself into the chair.

Young George in the corner is a sorry state.
I mind him sneaking past the checkie in the penny crush,
hoying his half-eaten snadgie in the projector beam,
aye and sitting in the front row to get sprayed with disinfectant.
Look at him, still wetting the seat, though now
it's not for fear of missing the Saturday serial.

Those were the days. *The Perils of Pauline, The Black Box,*
with Mr Martin's sound effects on the Vitasona
until they brought in Mirrorphonic Sound
and Western Electric, stripping out the gas lamps.

I thought the tunes were dead. All those years of babies,
washing, shopping, the making do when I was left alone,
turning my hands to working a till at the corner store instead,
hearing pleas from my daughter to give the past a rest,
grandchildren glued to their new-fangled colour television.

Garibaldi's Legs

They couldn't look me in the eye when they brought me here,
two suitcases and what I was wearing,
everyone out like a shot before I'd finished my unpacking.
Tomorrow, when I get my telegram, they'll all be round,
my own blood who never see me from one year to the next
will wear their fixed smiles through *The Studio Girl,
Sauce for the Goose, Chu Chin Chow.* I'll play them all.

Snadgie - turnip

Fiona Ritchie Walker

Adorned

I love to look at their rings, thin gold bands and tiny wartime
                                                diamonds.
The links in their watches lie loose on sparrow bones; sometimes
                                     the glass is cracked.

Old Mary's locket shows Joe was good looking. She thinks he's
                                       the plumber
though they share the same room, keeps wanting him to fix the taps.

I'm careful about what I choose, check out the families visiting
on Sundays. Mary's locket will fit snugly between her daughter's
                                                 breasts.

Back home, the ballerina twirls to a tune that's dying. I tip the box
                                              onto my bed,
wind her up again. Each ring glints with proposals, bended knees,
                                              chaste kisses.

After Life

Lately Al's been thinking about the soul,
hoping some small part might remain
body-bound when life is over.
Driving from the crematorium he wonders
if the soul can feel. Does Errol sense
his best friend's fingers
running through his crumbled bones?

When Al broaches this with Phillida
she rushes from the room crying.
That's what people like about his wife,
her compassion and caring.
Maybe that's why his eyes fall
on the advert, booking Errol in
for a blast of 3,000 degrees.

Al knew he couldn't lose with diamonds.
The ring sparkles on Phillida's finger
as they renew their marriage vows.
The priest speaks of the sadness
that best man Errol can't be with them.
Al smiles, runs his tongue over
the diamond stud on his front tooth,
marvels at the way heat can transform
burnt bones into every woman's best friend.

Fiona Ritchie Walker

Tonight, in candlelight, he'll kiss Phillida all over,
Errol's new-found phosphorescence
revisiting those warm, familiar places.

*In 2003, newspapers reported that human ashes heated to 3,000
degrees Celsius had been turned into diamonds*

Jericho

I must have done something wrong,
cut the carrots chunky not into dinner party batons.
His silence is a thick soup, coating my conversation.
I try to remember when his unspoken words
caressed my shoulders like a soft shawl.

> He puts the handmade glasses from Jericho on the table.
> The shop we bought them in was confettied
> pink, green and the blue
> we know we'd both like best,
> colour dripping down the stems like ink, like rain.
>
> We watched the demonstration, the way
> the man bounced the glass off the stone floor,
> clashed two goblets together like cymbals.
> *Unbreakable, ready packed for air travel.*
> *20% discount for you lovely people.*
>
> At the airport, security hand-searched every suitcase.
> A woman's bag slipped from her fingers.
> When she prised open the polystyrene packaging
> broken glass lay everywhere.

We use our glasses often, filling them with red wine,
handwashing and rinsing instead of stacking in the dishwasher.
Sometimes I hold one to the light,
check for faults, a thinning.
Any sign of breaking.

Fiona Ritchie Walker

Garibaldi's Legs

(for the head without a body in Blaydon Library)

It's the shape of your mouth that does it, that perfect arc,
the end of a penne pasta, al dente, a mouth shaped for passion
or smoke rings, if only you could find a cigarette.

A curve that draws me every time I'm in the queue
for library books, your stone face silently saying
where's the rest of me – body, arms, legs?

There's a place on my rooftop, Gari. Sheltered, high.
You could look out over streets and yards, both sides
of the Tyne, maybe spot your leg in a garden wall,
moss-trimmed knee in the rockery.

I'll drive us to the coast. Tynemouth, South Shields.
You choose. We'll find a restaurant,
Italian, I'll feed you spaghetti and red wine.
Help you to dance.

9:28 to Newcastle

Liz and Phil have spli' up.
She's upped sticks and moved to Brussels.
Fancy a night out there?

What's she doing with the cat?
It was really ancient.

How come she has a cat?

Got it when her parents spli' up.
Her mum was right frumpy
but must've cut it between the sheets.
She'd shag anything, did Liz's ex
when he wasn't an ex,
if you know what I mean.

We're out of the loop now,
don't know what's happening.
Suddenly you are your parents.

What about Phil?
He goes away on those outdoor weekends,
I bet those climbing women are up to it.

What happened to their greenhouse?
It had automatic doors,
he kept carniverous plants,
what happened to that?

Fiona Ritchie Walker

Was Phil at that wedding with the glam rock band?
I was well gutted, so pissed I yelled
Play Stonehenge from Spinal Tap.
I ended up dancing with this guy,
we both had our shirts off.

Are you up for some thong spotting?

Durham is the best view on the east coast line.
Except for Berwick. Look at her, she's up for it.
We should have gone to Hartlepool,
that's a great night out.

Sleeping With My Lover

Don't ask me for medical terms, all I know
is she burst in our bed, shedding herself
in shades of red and russet, ugly flooding
on the mattress. I switched on the light
to find a frenzy of re-decoration,
even the far wall stippled rose.

I like to think the end was brief.
She hated blood, cried the time
she brushed her teeth so hard
the spit ran red, dreaded
that time of the month, refusing
to let me see her, locking the door
while she hand-washed underwear.

The mattress was new, she chose it,
bouncing hard that first night,
testing for squeaks, pronouncing
it fit for loving. Last night
I stripped away clean sheets,
lay my skin next to her, woke
fondling a mattress button,
dreaming of her skin, taut nipples.
sucking blood from my own bruised lips.

Fiona Ritchie Walker

Beyond Durban

So he sees a spacious lounge,
three bathrooms, one ensuite.
And I see cracks down walls,
seven broken steps.

Viewing the mosquito net
he thinks romance.
I finger an angry lump,
start multiplying.

The maid instructs me
in how to stun snakes
and I wonder if it's happening
but the boerewors roll tastes real

and everyone thinks I'll live here.
They're planning a tour of the town,
will tell me where to shop,
avoid getting caught in the crossfire.

Between the bakers and the spice stall,
beside the man who shortchanges strangers,
I learn that the previous wife
took two years to settle in.

They say I must never make jelly.
It will collapse tier upon tier,
slithering into the snake holes,
drying on dust.

Garibaldi's Legs

I watch him shaking hands,
nodding yes. Feel myself oozing.

Fiona Ritchie Walker

Wrong Timing

Knowing that she has missed the 10:18
she still pitches up at the bus stop,

tells herself that in this city nothing
is on time, and miracles can happen,
though she ignores the tell-tale emptiness,
lack of fellow travellers and

knowing that the 10:48 might not come,
for in this city nothing is on time
and miracles are myths passed down
through generations, she peers
inside when the shiny car stops,
takes in clean-cut looks, thin-rimmed glasses,

yes, he is going her way,
three years as a student waiting for buses,
knows how she is feeling
and having made eye contact
and knowing the forecast is rain after midnight,
but in this city nothing is on time
and weathermen are not reliable,
she opens the door and slides in,

buckles up her seat belt, muffling
the click of his remote locking, fails
to notice the wrong route he is taking
until the street lights are fading and the 11:48,
the last bus, is winding, empty, past her house
where her flatmate is locking the door,

Garibaldi's Legs

closing bedroom curtains, knowing
that in this city nothing is on time and girls
are always staying over with boyfriends
and bad things always happen

to people whose names you don't know
when you read about them in the papers.

Fiona Ritchie Walker

On the Factory Floor

You may think I'm old fashioned but I like to wear the gloves.
Maureen says the touch gives her a thrill all day. She paints
the tips pink, holds the head close to her face while she's working.
On a Friday, when Gavin's coming home, I can see her top lip
                                                      sweat.

I am still on veins. Tim says I've a steady hand, know how
to build the best colour, that dull blue throb of expectation
that gets women going. Clocking off, I feel varicose,
thankful Steve likes doing it in the dark.

Small Things I Have Slept With

Today I am a moveable feast, taking my dead skin
to a different bed, depriving
my own dust mites for ten days,
though they won't go hungry.
I've left them a real treat, not changed the sheets.

Even now their mouths are filling up
with skin and sweat shed in restless dreams.
Hunks of me are setting off across the threshold,
I disappear through cracks.

On my organic pillow generations breed and die,
all smaller than the full stop at the end of this line.
No heart or head, they've given up on eyes,
rely on eight hairy legs to travel
between sheets and beyond,
finding new ecosystems. Madonna, the Queen,
the Pope, that street kid on the corner,
each of us on the menu.

Tonight the mites are dining out,
this hotel bed a smorgasbord of nationalities,
my every turn under the covers revealing
potential partners, high with pheromones,
hanging on every fibre.

Fiona Ritchie Walker

I wonder if they sleep and do they dream,
imagining themselves in hummingbird nostrils,
riding on the feet of army ants
until my earthquake turnings make their world unsteady.

Feast and enjoy, you skin-seeking arachnids.
This all-you-can-eat-buffet
will be power-showered clean in the morning.

Tie-dyed T-shirt

Boutique Elvira's were fourteen bob
so I bought cheap white
from Slasher Bill, Dylon from Boots.

The powder bled blue in the bowl,
lay like a still pool while I took string,
smooth pebbles from Usan,

shells brought back from Benidorm,
tied them up with dreams
of frothy coffees at Cura's,

having money for the jukebox,
platforms from Hogg's shoe shop
and Miner's make-up from Woolworth's,

late-night dancing at the Locarno,
longing to be walked home,
to stand in our close and be kissed.

I soaked them all in denim blue, never found
the Marigolds, used bare hands to pound it out
and rinse again until the water ran clear

and I could cut the string and find
my own tie-dyed
to wear to the beach, the baths,

Fiona Ritchie Walker

the barbecue where he would open
my hot tin of beans then walk me home
and one day months away

would ask to wear it and I would gladly
give it, imagine his muscles within it
then move on and forget

until a lifetime later
I'm passing Fenwick's window
and there's my t-shirt's twin

so when my husband comes home, nothing cooked,
nothing ready, I'm still crouched by the cupboard,
my hands stained blue by the shell.

Estuary Island

So it was silt, sand and a fish box
washed in by the North Sea,
but it was our den all summer,
cut off twice daily, hidden by dunes.

A season of sand castles, shells,
crabs' claws, dried seaweed decorations,
the little world we made,
burning salmon poles at the summer solstice.

That last night of the holidays,
two cans of Tennent's lager
between us all, everything changing,
him and me the last to leave,

piggybacking to a windswept shore,
his hands on my thighs,
the fullness of his shoulders,
a sudden storm, marram stinging

bare skin, red weals in the morning,
the rhythm of his south-bound train,
a serenade for charred wood on the beach,
a fish box floating towards the horizon.

Fiona Ritchie Walker

Girls I Like

They've glossy well-kept hair.
I can't be doing with messy,
too hard to cut out.

Best if they're not overlapping,
no sitting on a leg, foot poking out,
that kind of thing.

Best if they're pretty,
on their own, not in a crowd.
I don't do groups.

Magazines are better than papers,
they give a better cut,
just listen to my scissors.

It fills in time, like at this bus stop,
starts a conversation.
My fingers are never idle.

Finished ones go
in the Milk Tray box. Yes,
dip in my bag and find them.

Your wrist is so slender,
I'd love to cut round that curve.
Take one if you like,

Garibaldi's Legs

the rest will go on my walls,
neat rows watching me.
If you've got a minute

I'll show you. All of them
are about your age,
all glossy, like your hair.

Strip

He gets the man to machete the sugar cane into pieces
then pass it through the car window,
and she says, it doesn't look sweet,
so he tells her
strip it with your teeth.

She watches as he peels the brown and green,
revealing sticky sinews.
This one's ripe, he says,
now you try.

The cane is hard, her teeth sink in
but nothing moves.
Here, take mine, he says
and they swap.

She is watching his white, even teeth, the way
his tongue flicks between his lips,
the way he doesn't care
that his chin and neck are glistening.

There is a sweet darkness spreading down
the blue of his shirt and she says
you're a messy eater,

so he tells her
look at your own top, missy,
on the day that she learns how to strip.

The Language of Birds

These are the words you need to know
for spotting birds in Avalon,
for spotting birds on cliffs and bays
around the coast of Newfoundland.

Make way for yarry tinker ducks,
soaring scurwinkles and fillidays,
look to the sky for hagdens and bawls
and listen at dawn for the wobby.

The old man by the tickle mouth
tells of turrs and murrs and noddys,
how he swinged their down with a red hot iron
and roasted them black in Bonne Bay.

Forget your pigeons, crows and gulls,
the words you need sound like their cries,
the words you need will free your tongue,
they'll make your vowels fly.

Fiona Ritchie Walker

Night-time Breathing

Since your last breath I've planned your funeral.
How inconsiderate dying the night before my presentation.
I've tried to remember if your father's away, how to contact
your cousin backpacking in Australia: the phone bill will be terrible.

What to do with the house? Your choice, so I'll sell up this summer,
buy somewhere smaller, closer to the shops. I'll change the car
for something economical. And your books will go, clothes too,
though I'll keep that soft sweatshirt I always borrow.

What about the kids? Teenagers, all of them, taller than me.
Such a bad time to cope on my own. Must push away
thoughts of contacting G. Not fair to phone
after so many years, unless his wife is dead or divorcing.

All our dreams of whale spotting now gone, it won't be the same
not sharing it with you, and I wanted to grow old
with someone I knew, who would massage and touch me
in all the right places, picnic in the rain, you know, my kind of
                                                                             thing.

I'm stopped by a gasp, your deep echoing snore.

So not tonight, such a relief. I mould myself close,
your rhythmic breathing singing me to sleep.

45 Not Out

I have hitched helicopter rides in the Arctic,
remained calm at knifepoint,
eaten the cheek of a moose,
a duck's throat, a fish's eye.

These hands have held my children,
stroked cheetahs,
found the trigger, fired a gun,
been coloured gold by cloudberries.

The rose-red of Petra seeps in my dreams,
every summer the scar on my arm reappears.
How we found that beach is a mystery,
what I wore and what we did indelible.

At the crossroads
I reflect beyond wrinkles and grey.
Before the lights turn green
I'll have pictured that truck driver naked.

Fiona Ritchie Walker

Last Request

This was what he wanted
and us being dutiful daughters
we never considered anything else
although the digging was hard
and us living at sea level
we kept hoping not to hit water
which we didn't
and Annette
who was more holy than me
kept thanking God for small mercies
and each times she prayed
she passed her shovel to Marianne
for she could not talk to God with dirty hands
and Marianne for all her size
dug more than the rest of us
until we had a pit bigger
than a yard shed and I'd swear
it sent back our voices
echoing round and round
while Julia started the Chevrolet
and drove it slowly
down the makeshift wooden track
into the earth
with Pa whose eyes just would not stay closed
stiff beside her
his favourite pipe in his checked shirt pocket
and I could see it through the side window
kept my eyes fixed on it all the time
we threw earth over his beloved blue Chevy

Garibaldi's Legs

while Colette led us in singing
Going Home in the same key
as the swelling siren of the Sheriff's car.

"These intelligent, original poems are an absolute delight. Ritchie Walker explores the landscape of relationships and Scottishness with a warm, acute eye. Her poetry is full of love and laughter, but is never twee. Here is one of the freshest voices to be found in the North East."

– Julia Darling

ISBN 0 906228 96 4
price £6.00